BRYCG - GATA

For most people who come into Leeds City Centre, Briggate has one overwhelming function — shopping! Flanked by leading stores, Leeds High Street has a constant bustle all day long as young and old, families and individuals, all hunt for every variety of clothing, gifts and leisure goods. Such is their hurry that they hardly ever look above shop window level, or venture into any of the nearby yards. This guide is intended to remedy this situation by pointing out a selection of Briggate's more interesting features.

It is surprising how events of long ago can still shape our lives today. When Ralph Paynel inherited Leeds around 1200 he found that his family had already given away the main village, which stretched the length of Kirkgate, leaving him with very little income. To solve this problem he established a very large 'new town' in 1207. This had a huge central market area with thirty plots for houses, shops and gardens extending on both sides to back lanes. This market place later became known as Briggate, **brycg** being the Old English word for bridge, and **gata** the Old Norse for a way or a street. Vicar Lane, the back lane to the east, lay alongside the vicarage, while Lands Lane, the back lane to the west, separated the borough from the open fields of the manor of Leeds. This symmetrical plan provided Leeds with a sound geometrical base for its future expansion, enabling it to develop its present efficient grid pattern of streets, which contrasts greatly to the random pattern found in many other towns.

As a market, Briggate was most prosperous in the early 18th century. Lower Briggate, lined by wealthy merchants' houses, had the world's largest market in woollen cloth, the same stalls being taken over later in the day by numerous craftsmen. Further up Briggate — flanked by hotels, inns and shops — came the stalls of the fruit dealers, then the market for milch cows, the fish stalls and then the Moot Hall, with the butchers' shambles to one side, and the wool market to the other. Next came the market cross for poultry and dairy products, followed by the corn market and the horse fair.

As Leeds prospered, the plots along Briggate began to be filled in with housing and business premises, while the market activities were removed to a number of separate cloth halls, corn exchanges and market halls, so that the whole street became free for traffic by the 1830s. In the course of further expansion, some of the yards were demolished to make way for new streets, for new arcades of shops, and later for new department stores, but throughout these changes Briggate has always continued its 800-year tradition as the principal shopping street of Leeds and West Yorkshire.

Briggate was closed to private vehicles in 1994 and fully pedestrianised in 1997. Now, after over a decade of redevelopment and high quality conservation work, and with the installation of new paving, lighting and seating, Briggate looks and feels better than it has ever done before. It is now well worth visiting just for its own sake, either during the busy weekday periods, or in the more peaceful early evenings. It is home to stylish shops and cafes and bustles with the lively sights and sounds of street entertainers.

The Walk

The walk starts at Leeds Bridge, the historic entrance to Briggate over the River Aire. Crossing the junction with Swinegate and The Calls, it then goes up the left (west) side of the street, and returns back down the right, making excursions to both sides in order to visit some of its most interesting locations.

1. Leeds Bridge

When Maurice Paynel laid out Briggate in 1207, tradition has it that the River Aire was then crossed only by a ferry. There certainly was a bridge here by the late 14th century, supposedly built with stones taken from the ruined 'castle' or moated manor house at the west end of Boar Lane. From here cannon balls rained down on Briggate on 23rd January 1643 during the Civil War as Parliamentary forces attacked Leeds from the south. The bridge was also used as a cloth market where the local clothiers displayed their woollen cloth for sale on the parapets every Tuesday and Saturday morning up to 1684, when it was removed to Lower Briggate. To cope with the increasing volume of traffic, the stone bridge was widened in 1730, 1760 and 1796, eventually being demolished in 1871 to make way for the present structure in cast iron, opened on 9th July 1873. It has a single arched span of 102ft 6inches supporting a 60ft wide roadway.

CIVIC TRUST LEEDS
LOUIS LE PRINCE
Louis Aimé August Le Prince came to Leeds in 1866 where he experimented in cinematography. In 1888 he patented a one-lens camera with which he filmed Leeds Bridge from this British Waterways building. These were probably the world's first successful moving pictures.

It is from the upper windows of the Georgian house at the south-east corner of the bridge in October 1888 that Louis le Prince photographed the world's first moving pictures using a single-lens camera.

Walk along the left side of the bridge and take the pedestrian crossing to the Golden Lion.

2. The Golden Lion has provided hospitality for travellers for centuries, for here stood the ferry house before Leeds Bridge was built in the 1300s. In the 1780s, when Samuel Vincent was landlord, daily coach services departed from here to York and Manchester but even when this trade was taken over by the railways the hotel continued to prosper, being rebuilt in its present form around 1880.

CIVIC TRUST LEEDS

E.J. ARNOLD & SON LTD

Britain's leading educational suppliers and printers was established in this Georgian merchant's house No.3 Briggate in 1870. Its warehouse and factory was in Blayd's Yard.

3. Blayds' Yard The three shops just up Briggate from the Golden Lion occupy the impressive early 18th century house of the Blayds family, one of the town's major cloth-merchant, banking and mayoral dynasties. Note the fine cornice at eaves level, and the way the central section stands slightly forward from the sides, both typical features of this period. It is well worthwhile to walk through the central archway into Blayds' Yard, noting the blue plaque to the printers and educational publishers E. J. Arnold which occupied the building on the south side of the yard. The Georgian buildings on its north side were originally connected with the cloth finishing and trading activities which played such an essential part in Leeds' remarkable economic success, they have now been sympathetically refurbished for modern use.

Return to Briggate and continue up, under the railway bridge, turning first left after the Viaduct Hotel, and then first right.

4. Trevelyan Square occupies the site of the former White Horse coaching inn. By the 1970s the old industrial and office premises around White Horse Street were falling into dereliction, and constituted an eyesore both from Boar Lane and from the railway line, but in 1992 these were totally redeveloped. The open square, surrounded by some of the best modern buildings in Leeds, is a pleasant oasis amidst the bustle of the busy city. The remarkable Talbot Hounds fountain was originally commissioned by Joseph Edwards in 1850 for the courtyard of his massive and grim Castle Carr at the head of Luddenden Dean beyond Halifax.

Continue up to Boar Lane, and look across to Holy Trinity Church but do not attempt to cross this busy road at this point.

5. Holy Trinity Church was built in 1723-7 to the designs of William Etty of York to provide a fine, elegant place of Anglican worship for the wealthy merchants of Leeds who, along with Lady Elizabeth Hastings of Ledston Hall, provided funds for its erection. Originally its tower terminated in a square wooden spire topped with a weather vane in the form of a golden fleece, but in 1839 this was replaced by the present spire designed by R. D. Chantrell of Leeds. The interior, with its giant Corinthian columns and fine plasterwork, is well worth a visit.

Now walk to the right, along Boar Lane, passing the Marriott Hotel

REINHARDT'S
YARD
ROSE & CROWN YARD
The Rose and Crown Inn
SHIP INN YARD
The Ship Inn
ANGEL INN YARD
The Angel Inn
GREEN'S COURT
WHEAT SHEAF YARD
The Wheat Sheaf Inn
The Leopard Inn
WILLIAM IV YARD
William 4th Inn
MINOR & SCURR'S YARD
PACK HORSE YARD
The Pack Horse Inn
TURK'S HEAD YARD
The Turk's Head Inn
UPTON'S YARD
The Leeds Times Office
HARDWICK'S YARD
WOOD'S YARD
NELSON'S YARD
The Bull and Bell Inn
SHERWOOD'S YARD
The George and Dragon P.H.
GEORGE & DRAGON YARD
DODSWORTH COURT
Temperance Hotel
COURT
BRIGGATE
Site of the Moot Hall (Formerly the Manor Court of Leeds)
The Bay Horse Inn
BAY HORSE YARD
WHITE HART YARD
The White Hart Inn
HIGGINS YARD
The Boot and Shoe Inn
WOOD STRE
The Boy and Barrel Inn
BOY & BARREL YARD
BLAKEWELL OX YARD
The Blakewell Ox Inn
FLEET
Fleet Street Shambles
Cheapside Shambles
Bazaar
CHEAPSIDE
Fish Market
PEACE'S YARD
FISH STREET
GOLDEN COCK YARD
The Golden Cock Inn
Site of the Old Prison
OLIVER'S YARD
NEWSOM'S YARD
Bull & Mouth Hotel
General Coach Office
OLD INFIRMARY YARD
FLETCHER'S
ALBION YARD
Albion Hotel
MARKET STREET
CUNDELL'S YARD
Central Market
B.M. 133.5
B.M. 126.7
B.M. 120.4
B.M. 121.0
B.M. 119.3
B.M. 116.7

Briggate's Burgage Plots

Until 1207 Leeds was an agricultural manor with a population of about 200 people. The village lay around the Parish Church and along Kirkgate. The villagers farmed large open fields with their ridge and furrow strips, grazed their animals on the uncultivated land and grew hay in the meadows.

To establish Briggate as a 'new town' within the manor, its Lord, Maurice Paynel, granted a charter establishing the newly laid out street as a manorial borough. The thirty building plots marked out on each side of the street were known as 'burgages' or 'burgage plots' and the inhabitants living in the properties that they built on them were known as burgesses. They were to be townsmen not farmers. They were to earn their living from a craft or a trade. They paid a rent of 16 pence each year for their plots. Unlike the other inhabitants of the manor, they would not be farming in the open fields, so they were each granted a half-acre allotment or 'toft' to grow food at the place today we know as Burmantofts (a corruption of 'burgage-men's tofts').

Briggate is one chain or 4 perches wide — 66 feet, the length of a cricket pitch. The burgage plots were 3 perches wide — 49ft 6inches. The depth of the plots varied between 10 and 18 perches. The longest plots were those which extended between Briggate and Lands Lane at the top end of Briggate on the west side. The burgesses were able to sub-let or sell their plots, so that over the centuries some of the plots became subdivided and their gardens became filled with properties of all kinds. Access was provide by the yard alleyways which were entered by the arched passageways through the buildings fronting Briggate.

The 1847 Ordnance Survey plan opposite shows the hundreds of buildings built in the yards: literally dozens of pubs, inns, houses, workshops, warehouses, and even slaughterhouses. Note in particular the butchers' shambles and fish market occupying Cheapside and Fleet Street and the buildings between. The plan also indicates the site of the Moot Hall in the middle of Briggate. Note too Wood Street on the right of Briggate towards the top; today its site is occupied by the County Arcade. Wood Street was a burgage plot converted to a street. It had cottages on both sides with yards running off including the Boy and Barrel Inn and the Boot and Shoe Inn. Above it is the Bay Horse Yard which today runs along the south side of Borders Bookshop.

On the opposite side of the Briggate you can see the Rose and Crown Yard with its inn, now occupied by Queen's Arcade. Almost all the yards below have inns—you can still eat and drink in the Ship Inn and the Angel Inn today. Below Commercial Street you can see the Turks Head Inn (now Whitelocks), the Bull and Bell, and the George and Dragon. All of these heaved with people on market days. A few gardens remained as late as 1815. In that year the bookseller and stationer, John Heaton, still lived in the house attached to his bookshop and warehouse at No. 7 Briggate, just above Swinegate on the west side. At the back of the house there was 'a pleasant little garden, where the lilacs bloomed luxuriantly and flowers could be reared'.

Opposite Page: An extract from the 1847 Ordnance Survey Map showing Briggate's yards above and below the junction with Commercial Street and Kirkgate.

6. The Marriott Hotel

This Italianate-Second Empire building, originally the Trevelyan Temperance Hotel, was erected in 1866-70 to the designs of Thomas Ambler, his client being Sir John Barran, one of the great pioneers of the world-famous Leeds wholesale clothing trade. In 1976 it was condemned for demolition, but fortunately a more enlightened attitude prevailed, and in 1994 it was splendidly renovated. Note the busts of Milton and Shakespeare over the doors in Boar Lane.

At the crossing turn left, across Boar Lane, and continue up the right side of Briggate for 100 metres to its junction with Kirkgate. On the way, look across at Burton's Arcade/ Top Shop and the classical Thornton & Co Ltd India Rubber Manufacturers' buildings which each occupy a medieval burgage plot; Marks and Spencer between them occupies two.

7. Briggate/Kirkgate Junction

Briggate at this point has seen many changes since it was created as a great market place in 1207. Between 1615 and 1825 the Moot Hall (the town hall and manorial court house) occupied the middle of the street, with butchers' shambles extending behind up to the market cross. Commercial Street was cut through into Briggate in 1806 to extend Kirkgate as a major route through the centre of Leeds.

Retrace your steps about 15 paces back down Briggate, and cross over and go into the first entry, Turk's Head Yard.

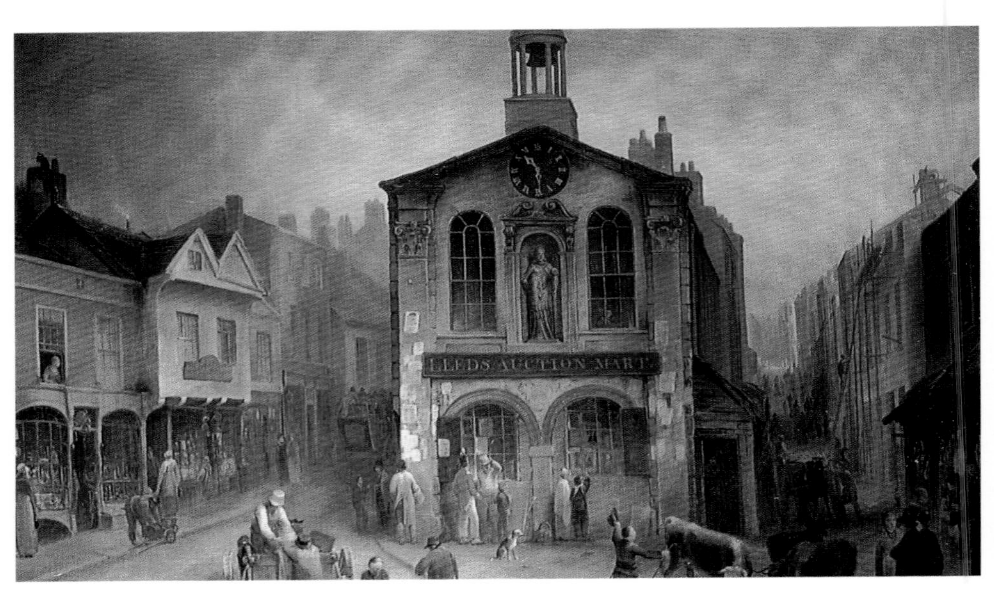

8. Turk's Head Yard

8. Turk's Head Yard was named after a former inn licensed in 1715, but since 1880 it has been occupied by Whitelock's First City Luncheon Bar, with one of the best Victorian pub interiors in the city, richly decorated with faience tiles, engraved mirrors, and polished brass fittings. Its dining area, which retains all the best traditions of English pub catering, is renowned for its roast beef and Yorkshire pudding. The buildings lining the left side of the yard were built as working class cottages around 1790, and feature the typical Yorkshire sash windows of this period, which slide across, rather than up and down. These houses clearly illustrate how the original 13th century garden crofts became congested with housing as the population of Georgian Leeds rapidly expanded within the constrained limits of its medieval boundaries.

Continue up the yard, through to Trinity Street, then turn right, and up, across Commercial Street, into the square which forms the start of Lands Lane.

9. Lands Lane It is hard to imagine this area some 700 years ago, when Trinity Street and Lands Lane were a narrow dirt track, with open fields to the left, and the back entrances to the gardens of burgage plots on the right. Commercial Street was created in 1806, but all the Georgian buildings here were swept away around 1900, and replaced by the present range of shops with their bright terracotta facades. These are well worth careful study, for their moulded decoration displays a wealth of fine detail.

Now enter Pack Horse Yard, the yard is half-way up the right hand side of the square.

10. Pack Horse Yard, formerly the Slip Inn Yard, was the home of Joseph Aspdin, who is commemorated here on a Civic Trust Blue Plaque. The yard was refurbished by the City Council in 1993.

CIVIC TRUST LEEDS

JOSEPH ASPDIN
(1778 - 1855)

Portland Cement, one of mankind's most important manufactured materials, was patented by Joseph Aspdin, a Leeds Bricklayer, on 21 October 1824. Aspdin lived in this yard (then called Slip Inn Yard) and first sold his cement in Angel Inn Yard.

Continue down the yard, through the Pack Horse Inn (rebuilt in the 1990s), then look backwards, up to its highest gable.

Here will be seen a Templar cross with two pairs of arms, recovered from the old building. Its purpose was to show that this was a Knight Templar property in the 13th century, and, as such, was able to claim a number of special privileges.

Continue down the yard, emerging into Briggate, then turn left, and left again, into;

11. Albion Place This street was only broken through into Briggate in the opening years of the 20th century, and so most of its fine buildings are Edwardian, the best being the Burmantofts faience block running up the right hand side of the street from Briggate. Its architect, Percy Robinson, was a Leeds historian, author of *Relics of Old Leeds* and *Leeds Old and New*.

Regrettably the adjacent block, which turns the corner into Lands Lane, was destroyed by fire but, as rebuilt in 1981, it provides an excellent example of how a building can be designed to admirably maintain the character of its surroundings, without slavishly copying every period detail.

At the junction of Albion Place with Lands Lane stands:

12. Leeds Church Institute

This useful organisation was formed in 1857 as part of the Rev. W. F. Hook's energetic promotion of Anglicanism in Leeds. The present building, designed in lively Gothic style by R. L. Adams in 1866-8, provided handsome accommodation for both religious and general educational classes, various church organisations, and a repository of hymnals for the popular Whitsuntide Walks. Notice how the pointed Gothic arches on the ground floor have now been skilfully used to provide unusual modern shop windows.

Turn right, up Lands Lane, and look for the first entry on the right, immediately at the far end of the broad redbrick and faience façade of the former 1922 Scala cinema.

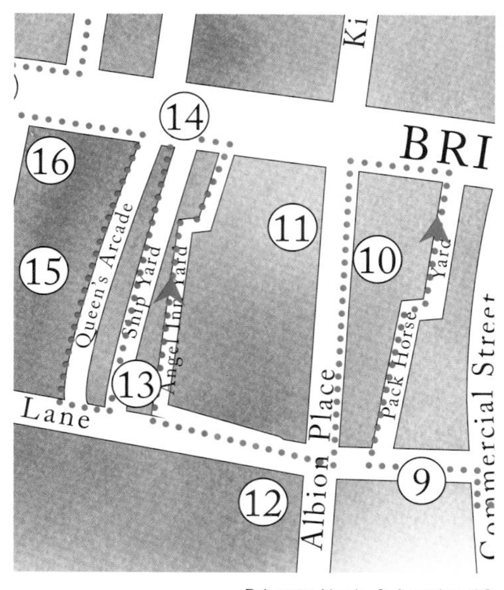

13. The Angel Inn Yard

If time allows, turn right off Lands Lane and proceed down the Angel Inn Yard, where Aspdin first sold his Portland Cement. The amazingly large and imposing late 18th century Angel Inn fronting the small square half way down the yard shows how in demand space was in these yards during the Georgian period. Survivals of this kind are very rare and its renovation was a major achievement in the battle to conserve the essential character of the Briggate yards.

Continue into Briggate, cross over the street and stand with your back to Harvey Nichols and look back to see clearly, even today, the distinct uniform 49ft 6inches widths of the medieval burgage plot revealed by the upper storeys of the buildings-Curry's one plot, the rendered Art Deco USC shop and Thornton's Arcade two more plots and between them four shops (including Queen's Arcade) occupying two plots. The section of John Cossins' Plan of Leeds in 1726 below shows the upper part of Briggate where you are now by the Market Cross. To the left it shows the ends of the burgage plots as they meet Lands Lane.

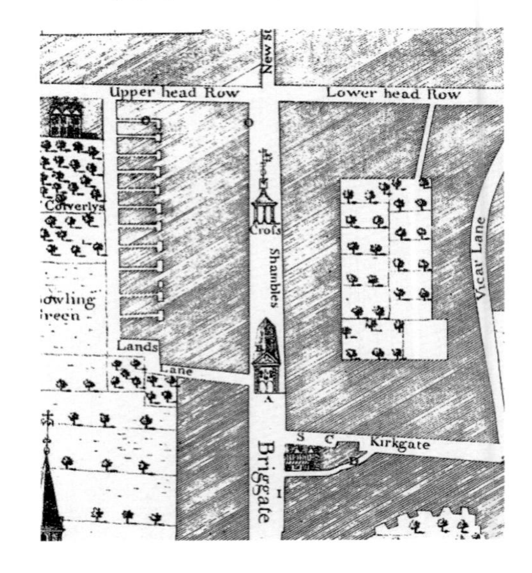

Next cross Briggate again and go into the next entry the Ship Inn Yard.

14. The Ship Inn Yard

This leads past the Ship Inn, and the plain back wall of Queen's Arcade on the right, back up to Lands Lane. This diversion gives a good opportunity to explore another of the original medieval burgage plots, although most of their present buildings are 19th century.

Having come back on to Lands Lane, turn right, then right again to walk down the first arcade to be visited on this walk. From the 1870s a number of developers discovered that greatly improved shopping facilities could be provided by demolishing the old yards, and rebuilding them as continuous rows of shops, all uniform in design, and protected from the weather by a high glass roof. Briggate can now boast the finest group of arcades in Britain, both in terms of their number, their size, and their quality.

CIVIC TRUST LEEDS
QUEEN'S ARCADE
Named in honour of
Queen Victoria's Golden Jubilee.
Built in 1888-9 by
Armistead and Proctor
on the site of the
Rose and Crown coaching inn
which occupied one of Briggate's
medieval burgage plots.
Architect:
Edward Clark

15. Queen's Arcade

15. Queen's Arcade occupies the site of the Rose and Crown Yard, for in 1889 the old hotel, joiners, tinners, plumbers, coffee, fish, tobacco and old clothes shops were all swept away and replaced by the present structure. To maximise the space, an additional tier of shops was constructed at first floor level, these being entered from the ornate cast iron balconies; above them was living accommodation for the shopkeepers. The arcade was refurbished in 1994.

At the bottom of the arcade turn left up Briggate, and left again up the next arcade.

16. Thornton's Arcade, the first in Leeds, was built on the former Talbot Yard site by Charles Thornton of the White Swan Inn in 1877-8. George Smith's Gothic Revival design, reminiscent of some great French cathedral, has many delightful details, including the florid capitals to the columns and the griffin heads on the roof. Best of all is the mechanical clock by Potts of Leeds in which J. W. Appleyard's figures of Robin Hood, Friar Tuck, Richard I and Gurth the Swineherd, all taken from Sir Walter Scott's Ivanhoe, each strike their bells every quarter of an hour. The arcade was refurbished in 1992-4.

At the top of the arcade turn right up Lands Lane, then first right down the next yard.

17. Swan Street is best known for the building which lines its left hand side, the famous Leeds City Palace of Varieties, the finest traditional music hall in Britain. Built in 1865 for Charles Thornton of the White Swan Inn on the Headrow, probably to the designs of George Smith, it still retains its original auditorium, formerly known to millions of television viewers as the setting to the immensely popular series entitled The Good Old Days. Swan Street was refurbished in 1993 as a pedestrian street complete with café tables.

At the bottom of Swan Street, walk into the centre of Briggate by McDonald's and compare the view with those of almost 200 years ago.

18. The Corn Market

You are now standing where the Briggate corn market was held from time immemorial. When an attempt was made to lure the farmers and corn factors away from here in 1825, the immediate response was to building a fine, classical Corn Exchange at the top of Briggate on the north side of the Head Row. Though the 1828 Corn Exchange has long since been demolished, the elegant block of shops built at the same time, shown in the 1829 engraving, still stands today on the right at the top of Briggate.

Now take a good look at the McDonald's building on your right.

Over the centuries many of Briggate's buildings have been demolished and rebuilt. But often owners wanting their properties to look more fashionable or to fulfil a new use, re-fronted them — timber framing giving way to brick — or modified their internal structure. The McDonald's building is an amazing example. The present street front was added in 1926 when the building was occupied by a high-class jeweller's shop. A substantial part of the main structure is in fact the eighteenth century brickwork of the house and shop shown in the 1829 engraving just to the right of the new block of shops. Incredibly, during the renovation of the McDonald's building in 1995 the timber framing of a two-storey, gabled and jettied, late-16th century house was uncovered in its north wall. Though covered over, it still remains today.

1. Leeds Bridge
2. The Golden Lion
3. Blayds' Yard
4. Trevelyan Square
5. Holy Trinity Church
6. The Marriott Hotel
7. Briggate/ Kirkgate
8. Turk's Head Yard
9. Lands Lane
10. Pack Horse Yard
11. Albion Place
12. The Leeds Church Institute
13. The Angel Inn Yard
14. The Ship Yard
15. Queen's Arcade
16. Thornton's Arcade
17. Swan Street
18. The Corn Market
19. The Headrow
20. St. John's Church

21. Kemplay's Academy
22. The Grand Theatre
23. The Grand Arcade
24. The Victoria Quarter
25. Queen Victoria Street
26. Fish Street
27. Kirkgate Markets
28. The First White Cloth Hall
29. The Assembly Rooms
30. The Third White Cloth Hall
31. The Corn Exchange
32. Hirst's Yard
33. Time ball Buildings
34. Clothmarket
35. The Royal Hotel
36. Lambert's Arcade
37. Queen's Court

Walk to the junction with the Headrow.

19. The Headrow is one of the most obvious achievements of the City Council's enlightened planning policies of the early 1920s. Before that time Upperhead Row to the left and Lowerhead Row to the right were about a third of their present width, but from 1927 the whole of the far side was demolished to make way for the new Headrow. This monumental thoroughfare, of truly metropolitan scale, was flanked by huge blocks of shops and offices, all sharing a uniform frontage designed by Sir Reginald Blomfield. To the left is the former Lewis's department store, which opened in 1932, then Headrow House of 1955, and a distant view of Cuthbert Brodrick's magnificent Town Hall, opened in 1858. Meanwhile to the right stands the former Odeon Cinema, opened as the Paramount in 1932, and long views down, along Eastgate, to the huge mass of Quarry House, completed in 1993 as the national headquarters of the NHS Executive and National Benefits Agency Social Security.

The Headrow is undergoing major redevelopment and refurbishment. The former Odeon Cinema looks resplendent as the Primark clothes store; while Lewis's, after a period as Alder's, has been renewed as three shops with offices above. Further west, the former Leeds Permanent Building Society Headquarter has become the architecturally stunning Light shopping and leisure centre and Radisson Hotel. Eastgate is to be the centre of the massive Eastgate and Harewood Quarter shopping and leisure development.

Now cross the Headrow, and walk up the left hand side of New Briggate, a new street created in 1868-9, to the churchyard gate.

20. St John's Church

with its plain Gothic detailing, looks early Victorian, but in fact it is one of the best early 17th century churches in Britain. It was completed in 1634 by John Harrison, woollen cloth merchant, one of Leeds' most generous benefactors, who also provided the town with almshouses and a new grammar school nearby. Although it is now a Redundant Church, the richly carved oak and fine plasterwork of its interior can be seen on most weekdays. Note the former Charity School, just within the small churchyard gate up Mark Lane to the left.

Continue up New Briggate, turning into the next short cul-de-sac on the left, to the cement-rendered frontage of Nash's Tudor Fish Restaurant. This was once:

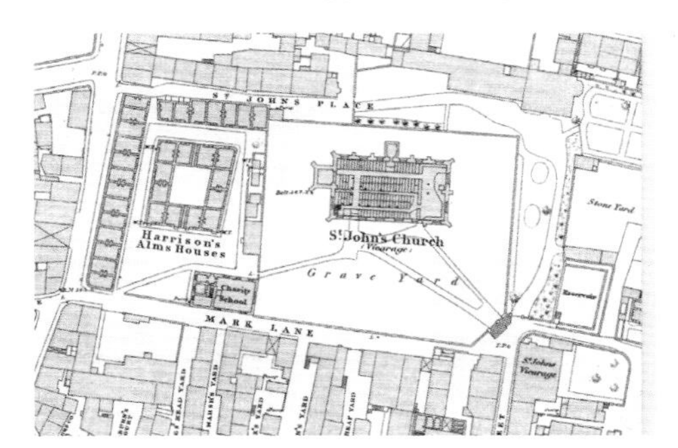

21. Kemplay's Academy

Built in 1720 in red brick with stone details as the home of Matthew Wilson, this house was occupied by Kemplay's Academy for Young Gentlemen during the later 18th and early 19th centuries. It was one of the best schools in the region, teaching both academic and commercial subjects with considerable success.

The adjacent half-timbered buildings are not as old as they first appear, having been built in this style around 1930 to complement the architecture of St John's Church.

Return to New Briggate, and look directly across the road to the Grand Theatre.

22. The Grand Theatre's

Romanesque frontage, with its 12th century details built in Victorian red-brick and stone, gives little indication of the scale and magnificence of the auditorium within, for the Grand is one of Britain's finest theatres. Designed by George Corson and J.R. Watson to hold audiences of some 2,300 people, it opened in 1878, and since that time has staged the greatest variety of theatrical and musical performances. Its reputation has been even further advanced since 1978, when it became the home of Opera North. In 2006 it was magnificently refurbished.

Continue up to the pedestrian crossing, then cross to the opposite side of New Briggate.

23. The Grand Arcade's

entrance is faced in both plain and glazed faience made at Burmantofts in east Leeds. Smith and Tweedales's design of 1896-7 was originally H-shaped in plan, but now only the southern arcade remains open, the other

being occupied by a nightclub. At the bottom end of the arcade another mechanical Potts clock can be seen. This one has a British Empire theme with figures representing Canada and India as well as a pair of knights to strike its bells with battle axes.

From the top of the Grand Arcade, walk down New Briggate, past the Grand Theatre and back to the Headrow, using the crossing to continue down the left side of Briggate and enter the County Arcade on the left. If closed, proceed to point 26.

24. The Victoria Quarter

as this area has been known since its excellent restoration by Prudential Portfolio Managers in 1989-90, was once a mass of narrow yards, gruesome slaughter houses and butchers' shops, but these were all bought up, demolished and redeveloped by the Leeds Estates Company in 1897-1902. Frank Matcham, recognised as the best theatre architect of this period, used a combination of Burmantofts faience, rich marbles, gilded mosaics, handsome cast and wrought iron and turned, carved and polished mahogany to create two streets, two arcades, and the Empire Theatre. The postcard above shows the development in 1904.

The County Arcade

is of unrivalled quality; note the fine mahogany shopfronts separated by pink marble columns with white Ionic capitals and red bases, the robust Burmantofts faience decoration above the cast iron balustrades, and the ornate glass and iron roof, which has mosaic figures representing the arts and industries beneath each of its three domes. The floor is an excellent example of modern mosaic work, forming part of the 1990 restoration scheme.

Half way down the County Arcade, turn right into Queen Victoria Street.

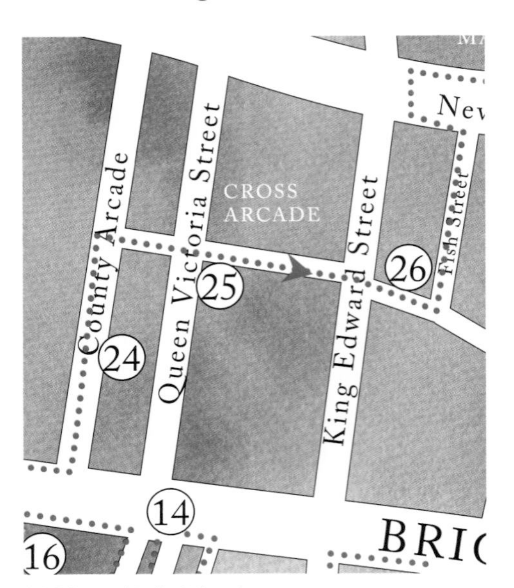

25. Queen Victoria Street

Up to 1989-90 this was an open street, but then it was converted into an arcade. Although every feature of the Edwardian frontages was carefully retained, it was decided that the new roof should be a distinctly late 20th century creation. Thanks to Brian Clarke's stunning design, Leeds now has Britain's largest, and probably most successful example of modern stained glass, the play of light through its richly coloured panels being a constant source of interest for those seated in the cafes below.

Continue directly across Queen Victoria Street into Cross Arcade, passing the former stage door of the Empire Theatre, which closed in 1961. The theatre was gutted in the 1960s but happily today its shell is occupied by the prestigious Harvey Nichols store. Proceed across King Edward Street into the narrow entry directly opposite.

26. Fish Street, which takes its name from the fish stalls which occupied this area throughout Queen Victoria's reign, is flanked by the former King Edward Restaurant on the left, and elaborately turreted shops on the right, both part of Frank Matcham's great Edwardian development.

Half way along Fish Street, turn first left, where the Golden Cock Yard stood, walk down to Vicar Lane, the medieval back lane for the burgage plots to the east of Briggate, and use the crossing to reach the markets opposite.

27. Kirkgate Markets stand on the site of the medieval Vicar's Croft. In 1822 the cattle, pig, fruit and vegetable markets were removed here from Briggate, various subsequent extensions and improvements being eclipsed when the magnificent New Borough Market Halls was built to the designs of Leeming & Leeming in 1901-4. It was completely refurbished by the City Council in association with Norwich Union in 1991-3 to its original splendour. If the market is open, take the opportunity of seeing the interior, with its fine cast iron framing decorated with the City arms in its arches, red dragons beneath its balconies, and original cast iron stalls. The clock

beneath the central dome was presented by Marks & Spencer to commemorate the centenary of the founding of their original Penny Bazaar here in 1884. With its 620 stalls, Kirkgate Market is the largest in Europe on a single site.

Walk along the Vicar Lane frontage of the market, then cross the top of Kirkgate, with its views down to R. D. Chantrell's Leeds Parish Church of 1838-41, and turn left, walking down the right hand side of Kirkgate, across Call Lane, to:

28. The First White Cloth Hall

This building is of major significance in the history of Leeds. Built by the local merchants and tradesmen in 1710-11, its purpose was to market special white woollen cloths, thus fending off competition from nearby towns, guaranteeing the rise of Leeds as the world capital of the wool textile trade, and creating the wealth for its future manufacturing and commercial expansion. Having had a variety of uses between 1756 and 2007, and stood derelict for many years, it is hoped that its restoration will soon be achieved.

Now retrace your steps up Kirkgate, turning first left into Call Lane, and left again into Crown Street, to the cream building which faces you.

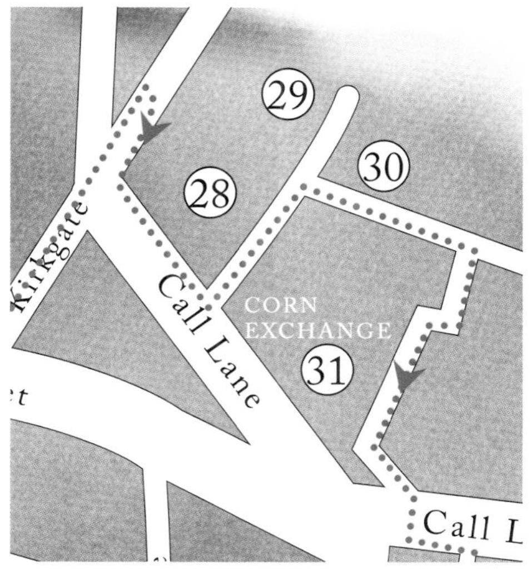

29. The Assembly Rooms

erected over the northern wing of the Third White Cloth Hall in 1776-7, were the centre of Georgian Leeds' elegant social life. Here, in a suite of magnificent reception rooms, grand balls, concerts and gambling took place until the departure of the gentry in the 1830s. Having served as a Working Men's Institute, builders' merchants, tobacco warehouse, antique centre and museum of Georgian Leeds, today the building is occupied by several bar-restaurants and a nightclub.

CIVIC TRUST LEEDS

WHITE CLOTH HALL

This superbly restored gateway belonged to the magnificent quadrangular market hall which underpinned the prosperity of Georgian Leeds. Merchants and 1300 West Riding clothiers met here on Tuesdays and Saturdays to trade in undyed 'white' woollen cloth.
Built 1775-76

From the Assembly Rooms, walk down to the nearby red brick building with the stone belfry over its entrance.

30. The Third White Cloth Hall

of 1775-6 was originally a huge courtyard surrounded by five indoor 'streets' of 1213 stalls where clothiers gathered every Tuesday morning to sell their unfinished and undyed cloth to the merchants. This trade ceased here in 1864-5 when the new railway viaduct sliced through the hall, but this gatehouse, surmounted by the cupola recovered from the 1756 Second White Cloth Hall, has now been beautifully restored as a restaurant.

From the Cloth Hall, proceed up Cloth Hall Street to Call Lane and the entrance to the Corn Exchange.

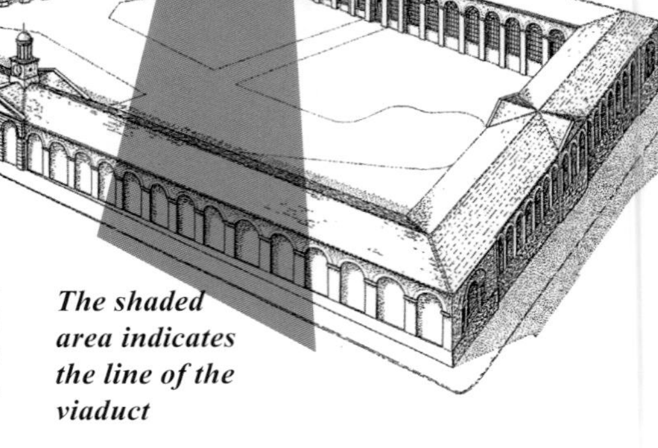

The shaded area indicates the line of the viaduct

31. The Corn Exchange

is one of Britain's finest Victorian buildings, being completed in 1864 to the Italianate designs of Cuthbert Brodrick, who was also responsible for both Leeds Town Hall and the Mechanics Institute (now the City Museum). Like them, it is remarkable for its strong architectural presence, and bold detailing cut in local stone. Within the outer perimeter of offices lay the Corn Exchange itself, a vast oval hall with windows inserted into its unique oval dome which were specially designed to exclude direct sunlight so that the dealers could accurately judge each sample of corn before completing a sale. In 1989-90 the whole building was magnificently restored as a shopping centre. New staircases now enable shoppers to gain ready access to both the basement level below and to the balcony above, where there are a wide variety of interesting shops and cafes, an excellent place to rest and take refreshment during a visit to the city.

On leaving the Corn Exchange cross the top of Call Lane, walk down its right hand pavement, and into the first yard on the right.

32. Hirst's Yard

has two buildings of particular interest, one being the first building to project on the left, a rare example of an early 19th century warehouse, which still has its original Yorkshire sash windows, shutters, loading door and crane for goods. The other is the former Whip Hotel, with its Victorian 'Tudor' entrance. This inn actually opened in 1830 in Bower's Court, the next yard down Briggate, only penetrating through into Hirst's Yard some thirty years later. This was the last men-only drinking house in Leeds, women only being admitted in the early 1980s.

Continue through Hirst's Yard into Briggate, stopping here to look directly across the road to:

33. Time Ball Buildings

This magnificent shop was operated from 1865 to 1990 by three generations of John Dyson & Sons, the city's leading jewellers, clock and watchmakers. Every day the two green balls were hoisted to the top of their masts, dropping precisely at 1pm so that everyone could check their timepieces against Greenwich Mean Time. The gilt figure of Father Time which stands on top of the projecting clock was carved by J.W. Appleyard of Cookridge Street.

After its closure, all the original Victorian interior, with its beautiful polished woodwork, etched glass, and brilliant chandeliers, was carefully preserved, to provide a splendid interior for its new use as the Georgetown Restaurant.

34. Cloth Market

This section of Briggate was formerly called Cloth Market, for this was the site of the world's largest market in woollen cloths between 1684 and the 1750s, when the new cloth halls were built. The clothiers who wove the cloth in the surrounding villages set out their unfinished wares on low benches erected along both sides of the street early every Tuesday and Saturday morning. The merchants then came along, carefully inspecting each piece, and whispering an appropriate offer, until they had bought whatever they needed. After the market had closed, the clothiers then carried their pieces of cloth into the yards of the merchants' houses, and the merchants' men went on to complete the finishing processes, and arrange for its sale and export both in this country and abroad. For this reason, this street was lined with prosperous merchant's houses, most of them dating from the early eighteenth century. The whole row downhill from Dyson's was swept away in the late 1970s, although some houses still survive on the east side of the road.

Continue a short distance down the left hand side of Briggate to:

35. The Royal Hotel

which had a long history as a coaching inn, accommodation for the numerous horses being provided on this constricted site by extensive stabling in the cellars, these being entered by sloping ramps. It closed down in 1963, being demolished some years later, and then rebuilt in 1981-3 as Regent House some of the first new city-centre flats, all pleasantly arranged around a private grassed inner courtyard. Great care was taken to retain its original appearance on to Briggate, but all is not what it seems. The original facade collapsed during the attempt to retain it; instead it was recreated — not in masonry or stucco — but actually in glass fibre. A gentle tap will reveal the truth!

At the end of the next property, look into Lambert's Arcade if it is open. This is not an arcade, but a yard. Access to the yard is restricted while it awaits refurbishment.

36. Lambert's Arcade

In the corner of the yard stands the last multi-storey jettied timber-framed building in Leeds. It once formed part of a much larger building erected here probably around the opening years of the 17th century. In the 19th century it was cement rendered to resemble masonry, and it is now weatherboarded, but originally it would likely have had its fine oak frame exposed to view, perhaps painted red with white panels, in the local tradition.

Now return to Briggate, and enter the next yard down towards the railway bridge.

37. Queen's Court

comprises the finest surviving Queen Anne cloth merchant's house fronting Briggate. Its central archway leads through, beneath the house, with its panelled rooms, into the court itself. Here the early 18th century buildings on the left were originally used for the finishing, baling, and despatching of the cloth to customers at home and overseas.

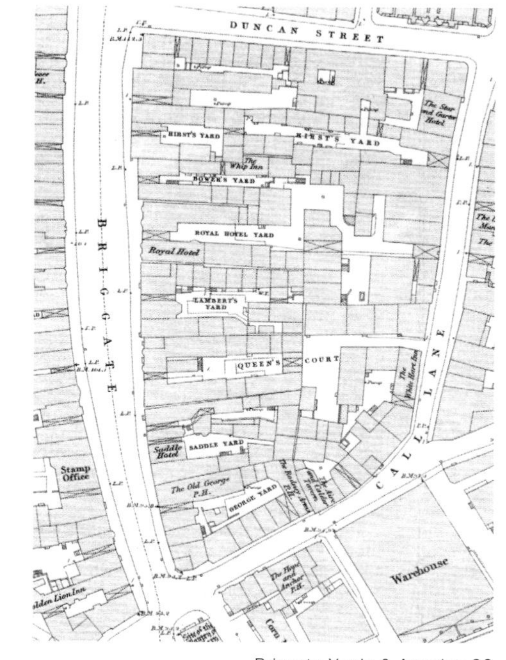

Those on the right probably being of the early 19th century, their loading bays in the upper storeys being for bales of wool, when the court was occupied by a number of wool suppliers or staplers. Later on, the buildings were split up into multiple use and eventually fell into a state of gross dereliction, but now they have been restored to house bars and restaurants.

This tour of Briggate finishes here in Queen's Court, but there is still far more to be seen in other parts of the City Centre and the Waterfront, for which guidebooks in this series are available from Leeds Civic Trust. However, you may continue through the court, then turn left and go back to the Corn Exchange, markets etc, or else return to Briggate, and walk down to see the river at Leeds Bridge. Over the bridge to the left, historic Dock Street takes you through to the attractive waterside Brewery Wharf with its restaurants and bars.